Examples of Gregorian Chant
and
Other Sacred Music of the 16th Century

Examples of Gregorian Chant
and
Other Sacred Music of the 16th Century

Compiled by

GUSTAVE FREDRIC SODERLUND

and

SAMUEL H. SCOTT

North Texas State University

PRENTICE-HALL, INC., Englewood Cliffs, New Jersey

PRENTICE-HALL INTERNATIONAL, INC., *London*
PRENTICE-HALL OF AUSTRALIA, PTY. LTD., *Sydney*
PRENTICE-HALL OF CANADA, LTD., *Toronto*
PRENTICE-HALL OF INDIA PRIVATE LIMITED, *New Delhi*
PRENTICE-HALL OF JAPAN, INC., *Tokyo*

FOREWORD

This collection was conceived primarily as an organized body of material to be used in classes in 16th century counterpoint. Since the basis for mastery of the technique lies in the ability to understand and to write in two and three voices, we have included 26 examples of two voice writing and 27 examples of three voice writing. For more advanced students examples of four and five voice writing have been included as well as larger, multi-movement Masses.

In the belief that there is a common body of techniques employed by the great composers of the period, examples from five different composers have been included. It is interesting to note that the basic similarities among them far outnumber the differences with which each composer stamps his work with his own personality.

The examples have been designated systematically by number in order to aid in ready and specific classroom reference. The first digit indicates the number of voices in the composition, and the second number simply indicates the position of the example in the series. Example 3-14, then, is the fourteenth example in the group of three voice compositions.

Identification of sources, commentary and translations are provided at the end of the collection.

No attempt has been made to use the half note as the inevitable pulse unit, for the student should develop the ability to recognize the proper pulse unit in spite of the conventional alla breve meter signature at the beginning of compositions.

Samuel Scott

Denton, Texas
July, 1970

CONTENTS

Examples of Gregorian Chant
and
Other Sacred Music of the 16th Century

Graduale Romanum

Libe Usualis

Solesmes

Gregorian Chant.
(Alme Pater.)

2

I (Dorian) Communion.
M.M. ♪ = 160

Pás ser * invé-nit sí-bi dó-mum, et túr-túr ní-dum, u-bi re-pó-nat púl-los sú os: al-tá-ri-a tú-a Dó-mi-ne vir-tú-tum, Rex mé-us, et Dé-us mé-us: be-á-ti qui há-bi-tant in dó-mo tú-a, in saé-cu-lum saé-cu-li lau-dá-bunt te.

II. (Hypodorian) Offertory.
M.M. ♪ = 144

Ad te Dó-mi-ne * le-vá-ri á-nimam mé-am: Dé-us mé-us, in te con-fí-do, non e-ru-bé-scam: ne-que ir-rí-de-ant me in-i-mí-ci mé-i: ét-e-nim u-ni-vér-si qui te exspe-ctant, non con-fun-dén-tur.

III. (Phrygian) Kyrie.
M.M. ♪ = 144

XI-XIII C

Ký-ri-e * e-lé-i-son. iij. Christe e-lé-i-son. iij Ký-ri-e e-lé-i-son. ij.

Ký-ri-e * e-lé-i-son.

4

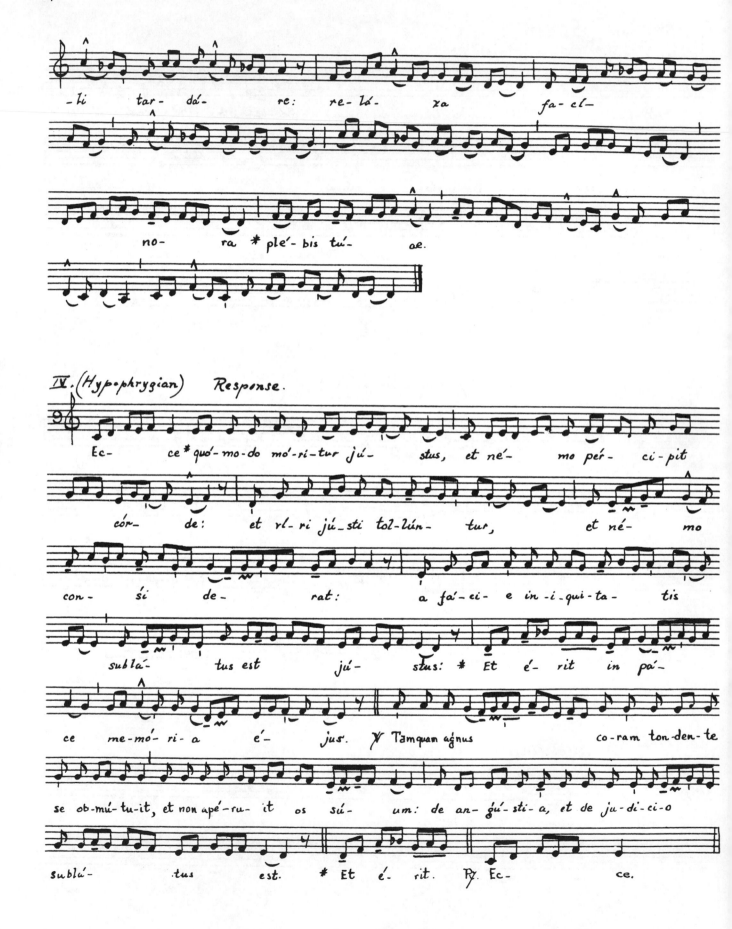

IV. (Hypophrygian) Response.

5

V. (Lydian) Sanctus.

V. (Lydian) Agnus Dei.

V. (Lydian) Antiphon.

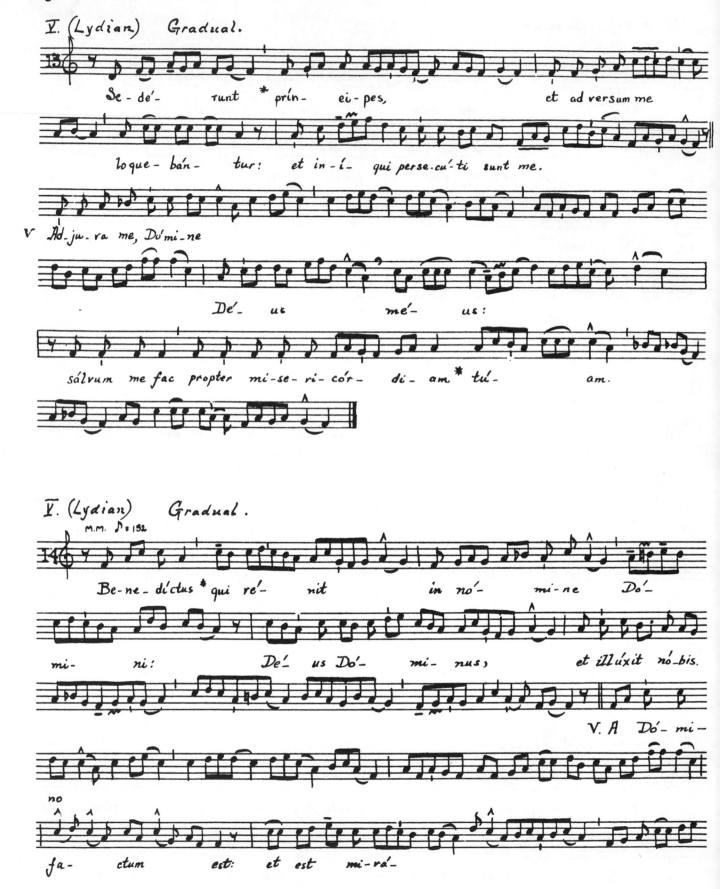

bi-le * in ó-cu-lis nó'-stris.

VI. (Hypolydian) Communion.

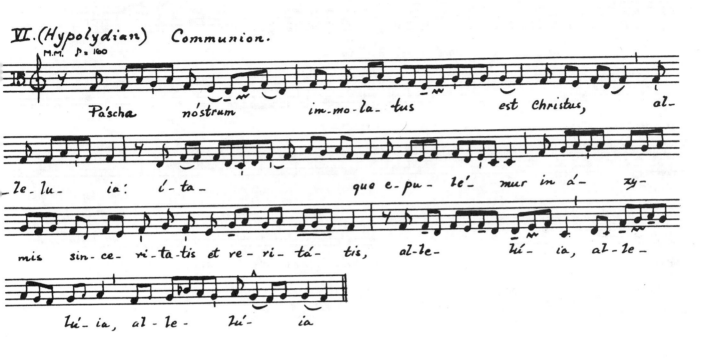

Páscha nóstrum im-mo-la-tus est Christus, al-
le-lu-ia: í-ta- que e-pu-le'- mur in á- zy-
mis sin-ce-ri-ta-tis et ve-ri-tá-tis, al-le- lú'-ia, al-le-
lú'-ia, al-le- lú'- ia

VII. (Mixolydian) Antiphon.

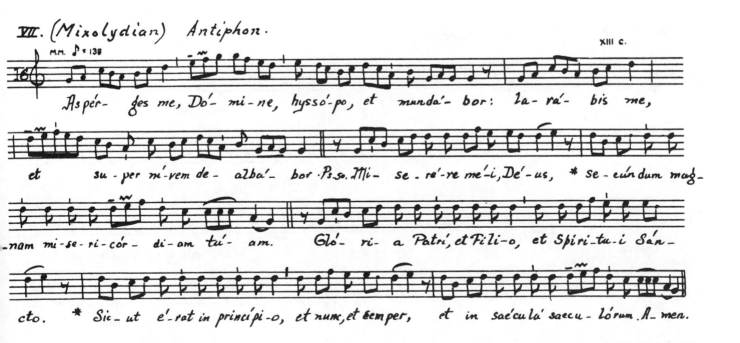

Aspér-ges me, Dó'-mi-ne, hysso'-po, et mundá'-bor: la-vá'-bis me,
et su-per ní-vem de-albá'-bor. Ps.50. Mi-se-re'-re me'-i, De'-us, * se-cún-dum mag-
-nam mi-se-ri-cór-di-am tú'-am. Gló'-ri-a Patri, et Fili-o, et Spiri-tu-i Sán-
cto. * Sic-ut e'-rat in princípi-o, et num, et semper, et in saécula' saecu-ló'rum. A-men.

8

VII. (Mixolydian) Gradual.

Qui se-des, Dómine *su-per Ché-ru-bim, éx-ci-ta pot én-ti-am túam, et ve-ni. V. Qui ré-gis Is-ra-el, in tén-de: qui de-dú-cis vel-ut ó-vem *Jó seph.

VIII. (Hypomixolydian) Offertory.

Pre-cá-tus est * Mó-y-ses in con spé-ctu Dó-mi-ni Dé-i sú-i, et dí-xit. Pre-cá-tus est Mó-y-ses in con spé-ctu Dó-mi-ni Dé-i sú-i, et dí-xit: Qua-re, Dó-mi-ne, i-rá-sce-ris in pó-pulo tú-

o? Pár- ce í-rae á nimae tú- ae:

memén- to Abra-ham, I- sa-ac et Ja'cob,

quibus ju-rá'sti da'-re terram flú-én-tem lac et

mel. Et pla-ca'tus fa'- ctus est Dó- mi- nus de ma-

lig-ni-tá'te, quam dí- xit fá- ce- re pó- pu-lo

su'- o.

VIII. (Hypomixolydian) Introit.

Spí-ri- tus Dómi - - - ni * re-plé-vit ór-bem ter-rá-rum, al-le-

--- lú- ia: et hoc quod cón--ti--net ó-- mni-a, sci-én-ti- am

--há-bet vó-cis, al-le-lú--ia, al- le-lú- ia, al-le-lú-ia.

Ps. Ex-sur-gat Dé-us, et dissi-pén-tur in-i- mí-ci é-jus: * et fú-gi-ant, qui o-dé-runt é-um,

a fá- ci-e é-jus. Gló-ri-a Pá-tri. E u o u a e.

Cantiones duarum vocum

Lassus

22

Tenor

2 – 8

Bassus

26

28.

Tenor

2-11

Bassus

Missa ad imitationem moduli *Puis que i ay perdu* : *Gloria*

Lassus

Missa ad imitationem moduli O passi sparsi : Gloria

Lassus

Missa super Frere Thibault: Credo

Lassus

Missa ad imitationem moduli Doulce memoire: Credo

Lassus

38

Missa Da pacem: Credo

des Pres

Missa Mater Patris: Sanctus

des Pres

Missa Super Frere Thibault: Benedictus

Lassus

Missa l'homme armé : Benedictus

des Pres

Superius

2 - 20c

Superius

Missa ad fugam : Benedictus

des Pres

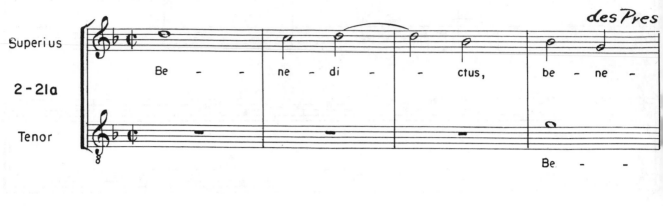

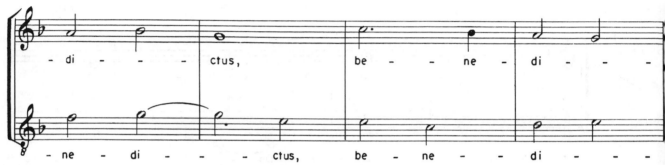

Missa Mater Patris: Benedictus

des Pres

-mi-ne Do - mi-ni, in no - mi-ne Do - - - - - -
in no - mi-ne Do - - mi-ni, in no - mi-ne Do - - - -
- mi-ni, in no - mi - ne, in no - mi - ne, in no -
- - - - mi-ni, in no - mi - ne, in no - mi - ne,
-mi - ne, in no - mi - ne, in no - - - - -
in no - mi - ne, in no - mi - ne, in no - -
- - mi-ne Do - - - - - - - - - - - - - -
- - - - mi-ne Do - - - - - - - - - - -
- - - - - - - - - - - - mi - ni.
- - - - - - - - - - - - - mi - - ni.

Missa Di dadi : Benedictus

des Pres

Missa La sol fa re mi : Agnus Dei

des Pres

Missa Mater Patris : Agnus Dei

des Pres

Missa de Beata Virgine: Agnus Dei

des Pres

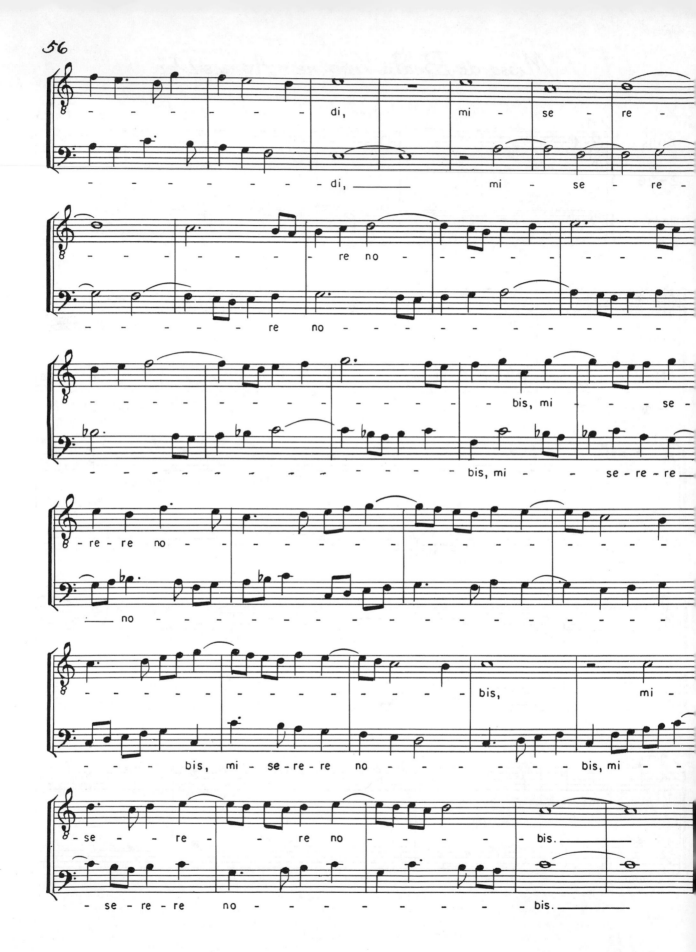

Magnificat Primi Toni: Et misericordia

Palestrina

Magnificat Tertii Toni : Et misericordia

Palestrina

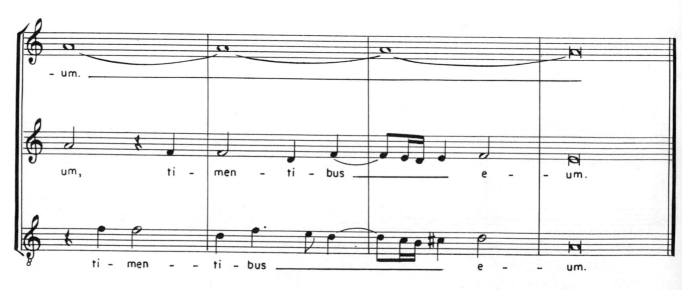

Magnificat Quinti Toni: Et misericordia

Palestrina

Magnificat Sexti Toni: Et misericordia

Palestrina

Magnificat Tertii Toni : Et misericordia

Victoria

Magnificat Secundi Toni: De posuit potentes

Palestrina

Magnificat Quarti Toni: De posuit potentes

Palestrina

70

Magnificat Octavi Toni : Deposuit potentes

Palestrina

Magnificat Secundi Toni : Deposuit potentes

Victoria

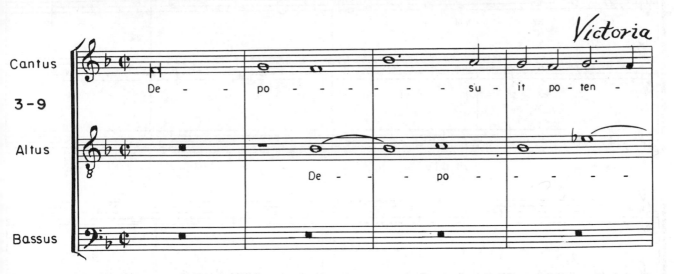

74

Magnificat Septimi Toni : Deposuit potentes

Victoria

hu - - - mi - les, et - ex - al - ta - - vit hu -

- vit hu - mi - les, et ex - al - ta - vit

- vit hu - mi - les, et ex - al - ta - vit

- - - mi - les, et ex - al - ta - - - - vit

hu - mi - les, et - ex - al - ta - - vit hu - -

hu - mi - les, et ex - al - ta - vit

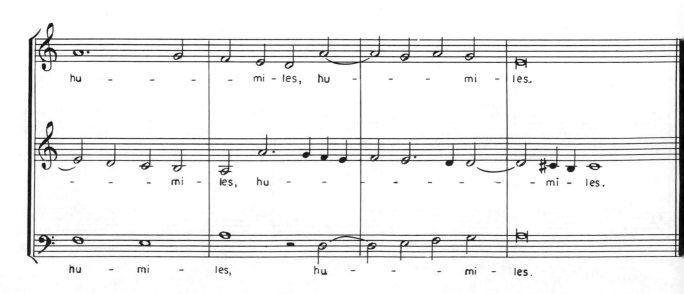

hu - - - - mi - les, hu - - - mi - les.

- - - mi - les, hu - - - - - mi - les.

hu - mi - les, hu - - - mi - les.

Missa Jam Christus astra ascenderat: Credo

Palestrina

Missa Spem in alium: Credo

Palestrina

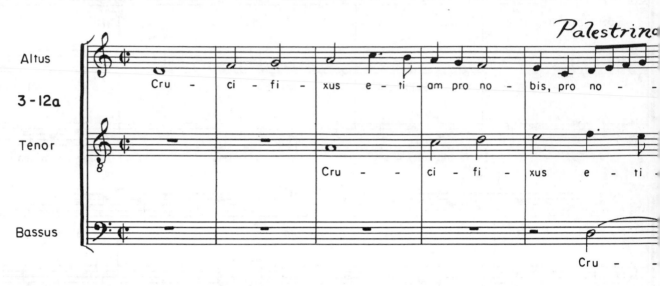

di - - - - - - e
se - cun - dum Scrip - tu -
se - cun - dum Scrip - tu - - - - - - - - - - - - - -
se - cun - dum Scrip - tu - - - - - - - - - -
- - - - - - - - - - - - - - - - - ras,
- - - - - - ras, se - cun - dum Scrip - tu - -
- - - - - ras, se - cun - dum
se - cun - dum Scrip - tu - - - ras, se - cun -
- - ras, se - cun - dum Scrip - tu - - - - - - ras,
Scrip - tu - - - - - - - - - - - - - - ras.
- dum Scrip - tu - - - - - - - - - - - ras.
se - - cun - dum Scrip - tu - - - - - ras.

Missa Repleatur os meum laude : Credo

Palestrina

Cantus

3 – 13

Altus

Bassus

- vos et mor - - - - tu - os:
- re vi - vos, vi - vos et mor - - - tu -
- re vi - vos et mor - - tu - os:
cu - jus re - gni non e - rit fi - - -
os: cu - jus re - gni non e - rit
cu - jus re - gni non e - rit fi - nis, non e - rit fi - - -
- nis, cu - jus re - gni non e - rit fi - nis,
fi - nis, fi - - - - nis, cu - jus re - gni non e - rit
- - - - - - - nis, cu - jus re - gni non
cu - jus re - gni non e - rit fi - - - nis.
fi - - - - - - - nis, non e - rit fi - nis.
e - rit fi - nis, non e - rit fi - - - nis.

Missa Inviolata : Credo

Palestrina

92

Missa ad imitationem moduli Susanne un iour: Credo

Lassus

Missa super Le Berger et la Bergere : Credo

Lassus

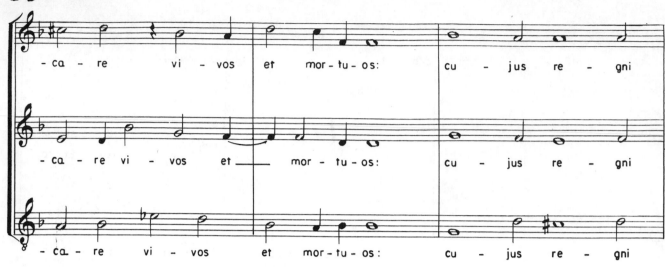

-ca - re vi - vos et mor - tu - os: cu - jus re - gni

-ca - re vi - vos et mor - tu - os: cu - jus re - gni

-ca - re vi - vos et mor - tu - os: cu - jus re - gni

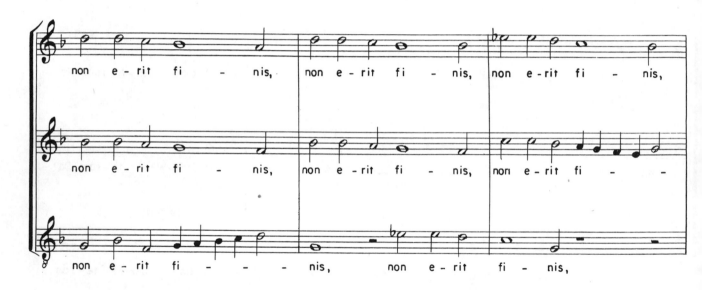

non e - rit fi - nis, non e - rit fi - nis, non e - rit fi - nis,

non e - rit fi - nis, non e - rit fi - nis, non e - rit fi -

non e - rit fi - nis, non e - rit fi - nis,

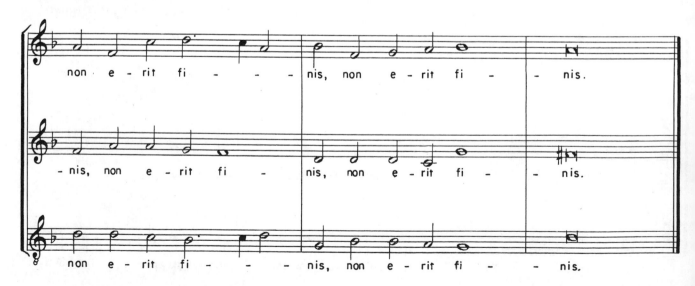

non e - rit fi - nis, non e - rit fi - nis.

-nis, non e - rit fi - nis, non e - rit fi - nis.

non e - rit fi - nis, non e - rit fi - nis.

Missa de Beata Virgine : Credo

Morales

Missa de Beata Virgine : Sanctus

Palestrina

Missa ad fugam : Sanctus

Palestrina

Missa Aspice Domine: Sanctus

Palestrina

108

Missa ad fugam : Sanctus

des Pres

Missa Brevis : Benedictus

Palestrina

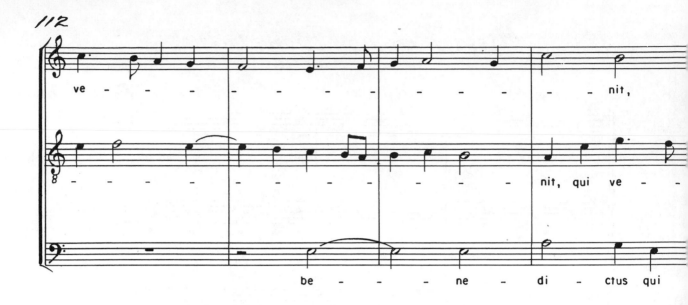

ve - - - - - - - - - - - - - nit,

- - - - - - - nit, qui ve -

be - - ne - di - ctus qui

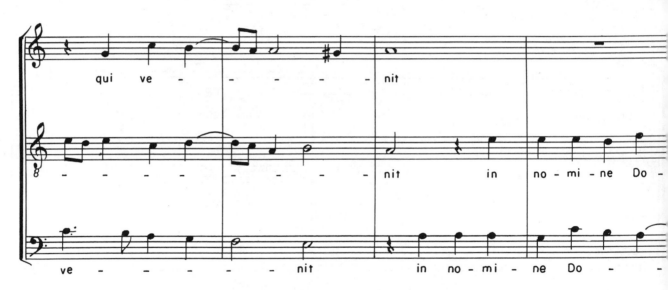

qui ve - - - - nit

- - - - nit in no - mi - ne Do -

ve - - - nit in no - mi - ne Do -

in no - mi - ne Do - - - mi - ni,

- - - - - mi - ni,

- - mi - ni, _____ Do - - mi - ni, in

Missa ad imitationem moduli Puis que i'ay perdu: Benedictus

Lassus

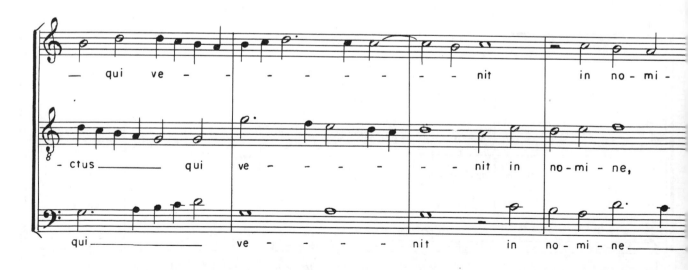

Missa Pro Defunctis : Benedictus

Lassus

Missa Mille regretz : Benedictus

Morales

118

Missa ad Fugam : Agnus Dei

des Pres

Missa Vulnerasti cor meum: Agnus Dei

Morales

3-27

Cantus

A — gnus De — — — i,

Altus

A — gnus De — — — i, a — gnus De —

Bassus

a — gnus De — — — — — — — i,

i, qui tol — lis pec — ca —

A — — gnus De — — — —

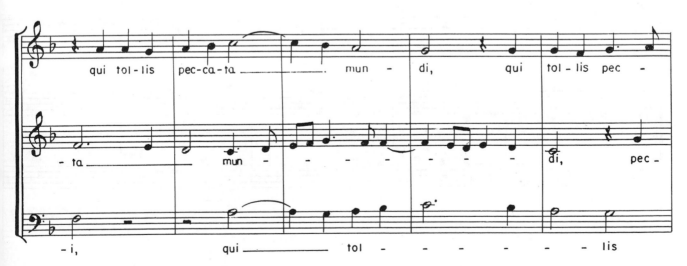

qui tol — lis pec — ca — ta _____ mun — di, qui tol — lis pec —

— ta _____ mun — — — — — — — — di, pec —

— i, qui _____ tol — — — — — — lis

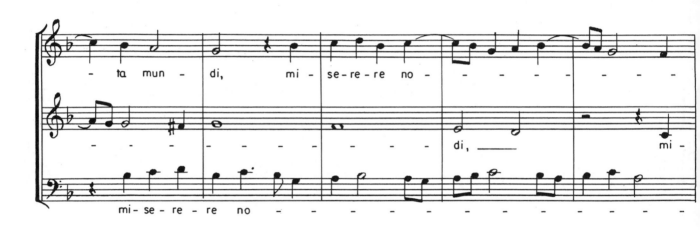

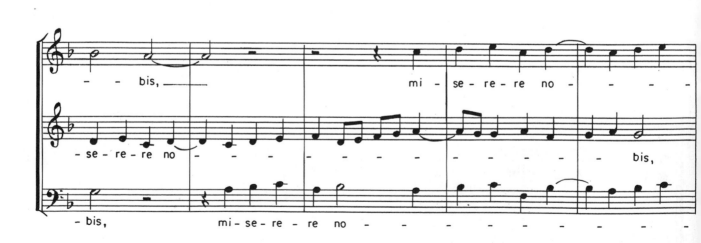

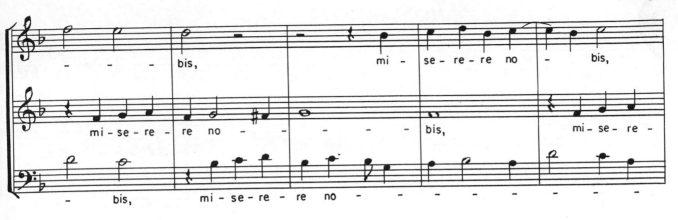

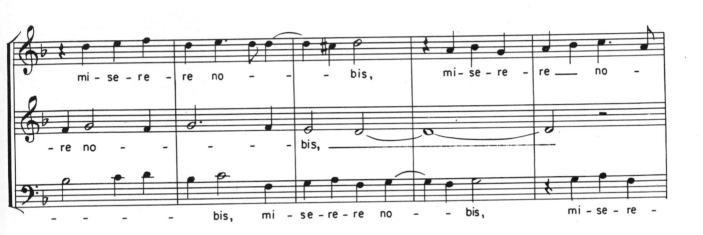

Mass: De Feria: Kyrie.   Palestrina.

Mass: Dies Sanctificatus:

Kyrie. Palestrina.

Mass: Gabriel Archangelus: Hosanna.   Palestrina.

Mass: Sine Nomine: Sanctus.   Palestrina.

Motet: Dies Sanctificatus.

Palestrina.

138

Hymn: In Festo Transfigurationis Domini.

Palestrina.

Magnificat.

Palestrina.

152

130

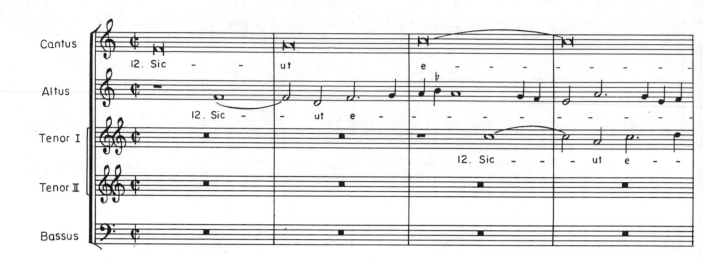

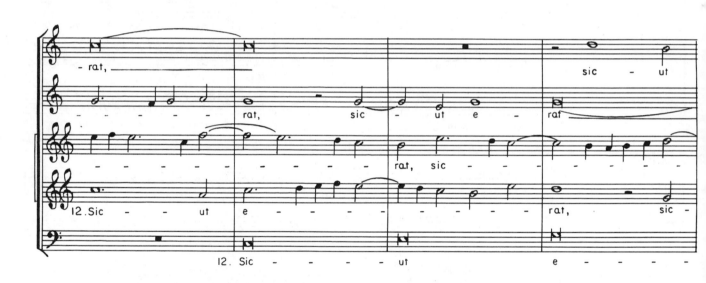

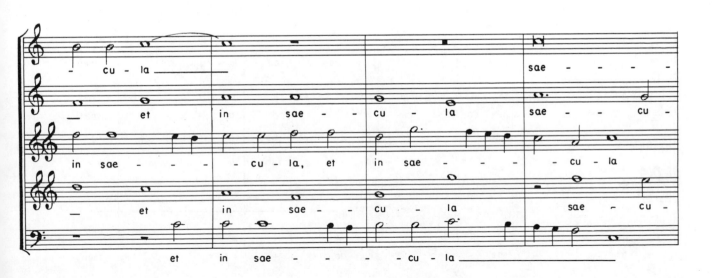

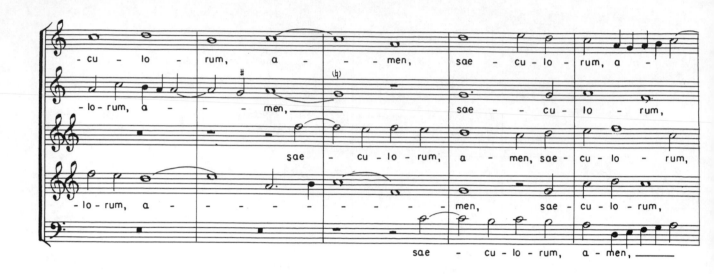

Mass: Sanctorum Meritis: Agnus Dei I and II.   Palestrina.

Mass: Petra Sancta: Kyrie. Palestrina.

164

30

Mass: Vestiva i Colli: Kyrie   Palestrina.

170

Mass: Vestiva i Colli: *Gloria.* *Palestrina.*

90

100

-ctus, tu so-lus Domi nus, tu solus Al-tis-si-mus, Altis-si-mus, Je-

_ niam tu solus san _ _ _ _ ctus, tu solus Dominus, tu solus Al _ tis-si-mus,

-ctus, san _ _ _ _ ctus, tu solus Do mi_nus,........... tu solus Al

san _ _ _ _ ctus, tu solus Do _ _ mi nus,....... tu solus Al_tis si mus,.......

_ _ ctus, tu solus Al _ _ tissimus, Al_tissimus,

_ _ su Chri _ ste, Je su Chri _ _ _ ste...... Cum sancto Spiri-tu......

Je _ su...... Chri-ste. Cum sancto Spi _ _ _ _ _ ri-tu in gloria De-i

_tissimus, Je _ su Christe. Cum sancto Spi_ri-tu,......... ... cum sancto Spiri-tu in gloria De-i

Je _ _ _ _ _ su Chri _ _ _ _ _ ste...... Cum san-cto Spi-ri-tu.........

Je_ su...... Chri_ _ _ _ ste. Cum sancto Spiri-tu in gloria De-i

Motet: Alleluia Tulerunt.

Palestrina.

Hymn: In Dominicis Quadragesima.

Palestrina.

Hymn: In Dominicis Qudragesima.

Palestrina.

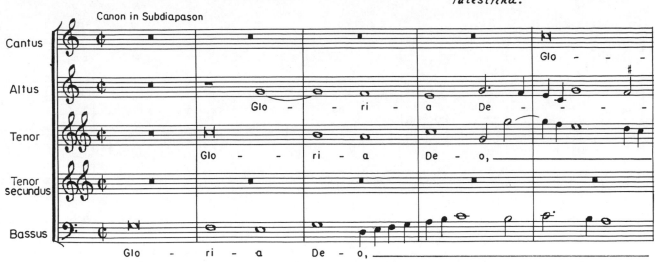

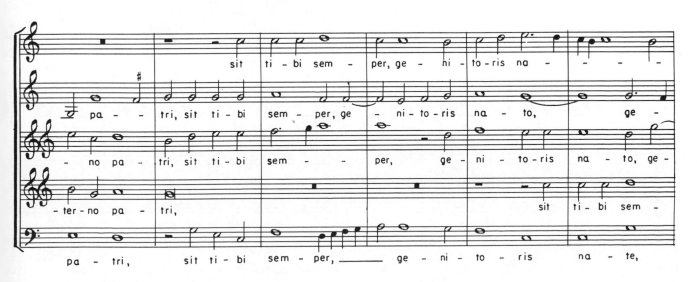

Offertory: Laudate Dominum.

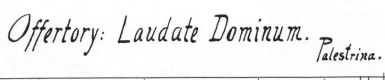

Palestrina.

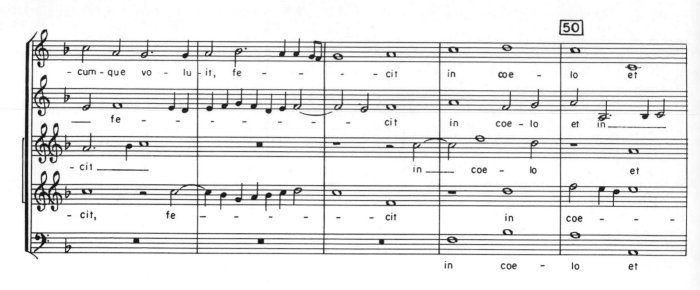

Offertory: Improperium. Palestrina.

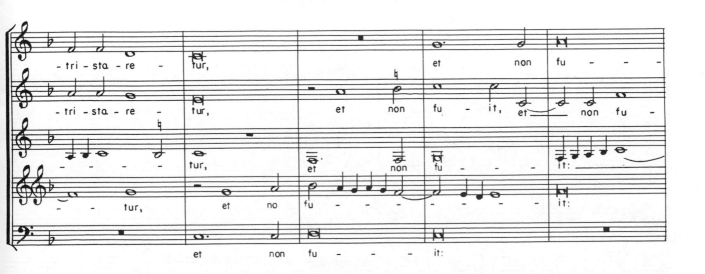

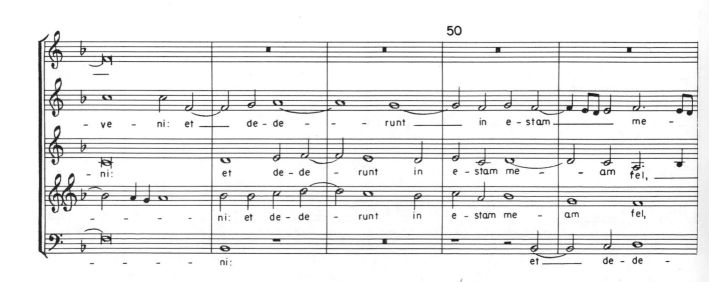

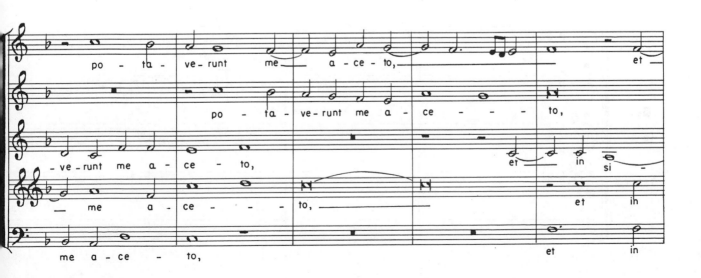

Offertory: Exaltabo Te.   Palestrina.

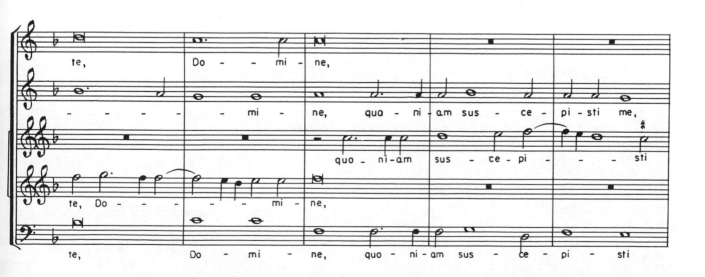

204

Litaniae de Beata Virgine Maria.

Palestrina.

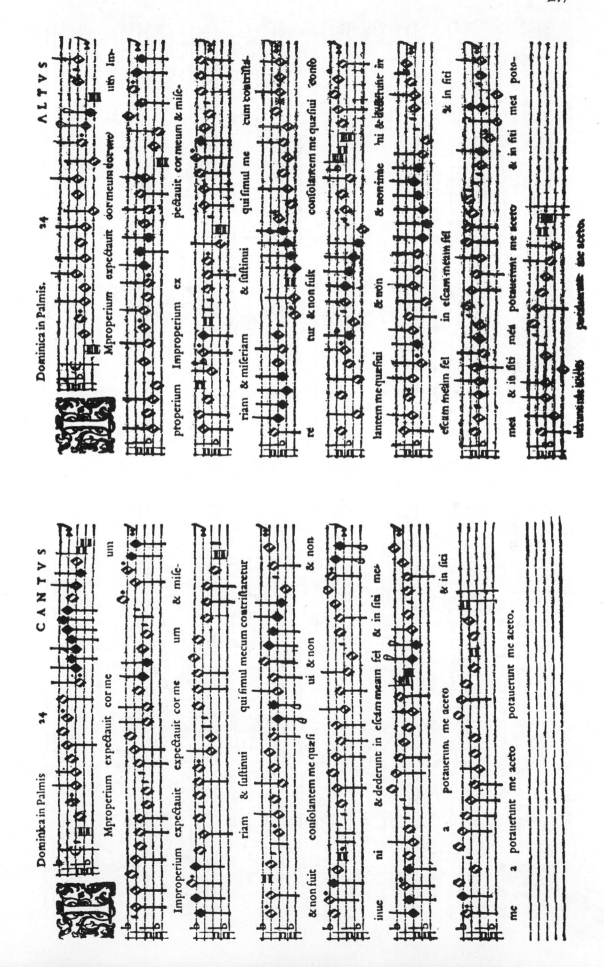

212

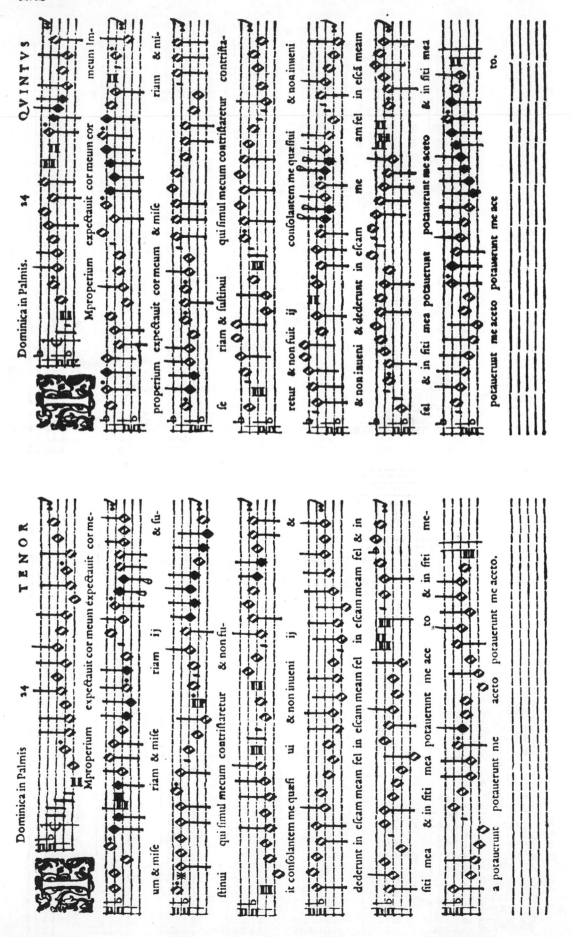

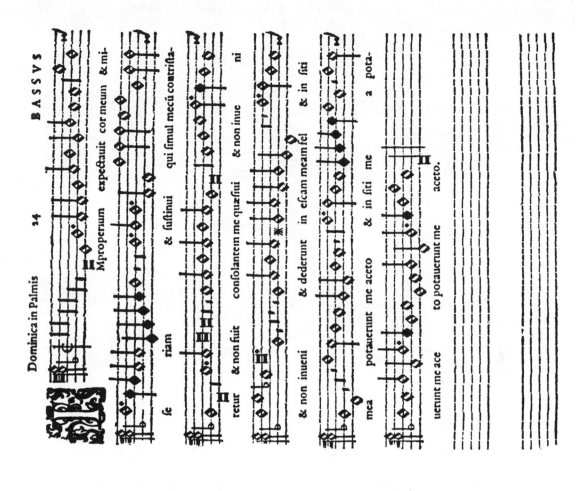

Mass: Ad Fugam: Kyrie.   *Palestrina.*

Mass: Ad Fugam: Benedictus. Palestrina.

Mass: Ad Fugam: Agnus Dei.   Palestrina.

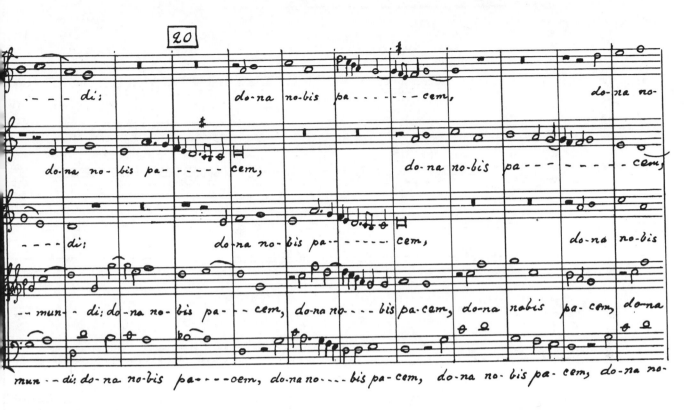

Mass: L'homme armé

Kyrie

Palestrina.

Gloria in excelsis Deo.

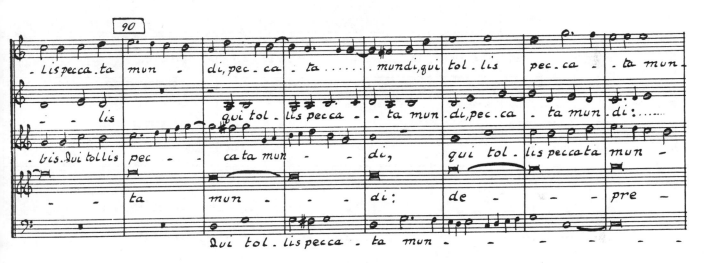

228

Credo in unum Deum.

230

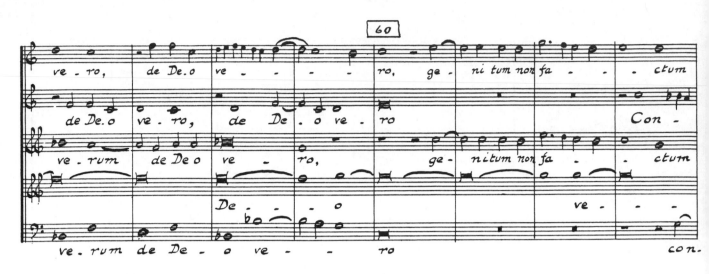

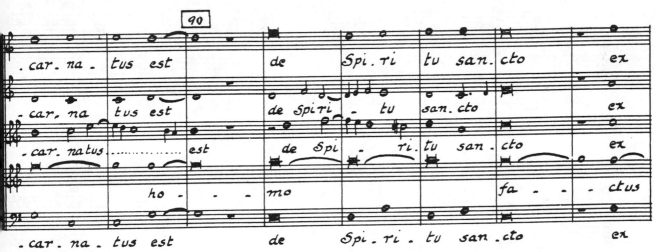

234

236

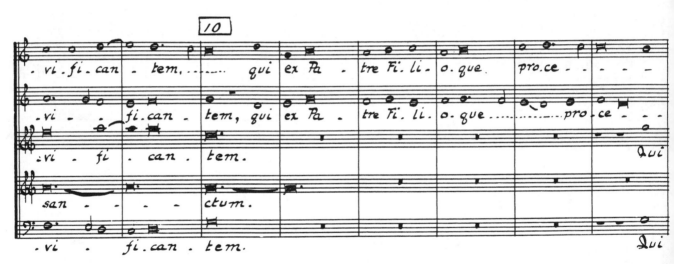

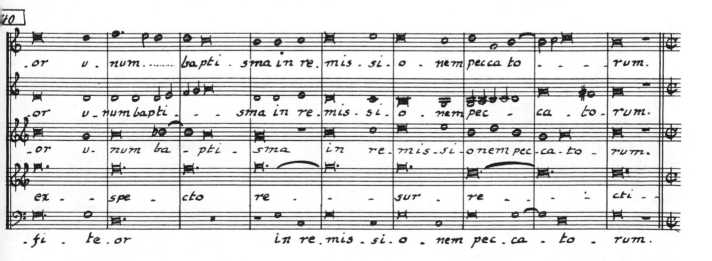

Sanctus

Hosanna

Benedictus

Agnus Dei I

246

20

30

40

Agnus Dei. II.

Mass: Ut Re Mi Fa Sol La: Kyrie

Palestrina

Gloria in excelsis Deo

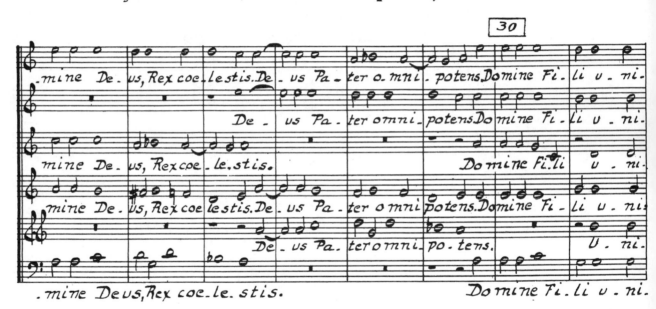

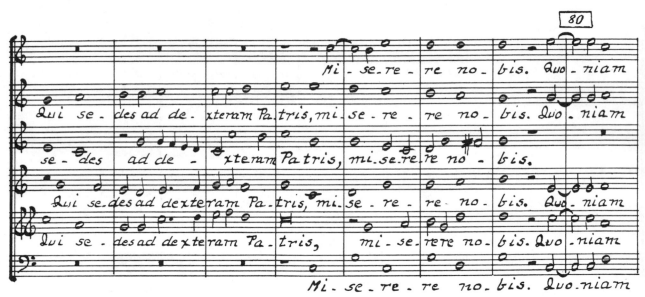

258

Credo in unum Deum.

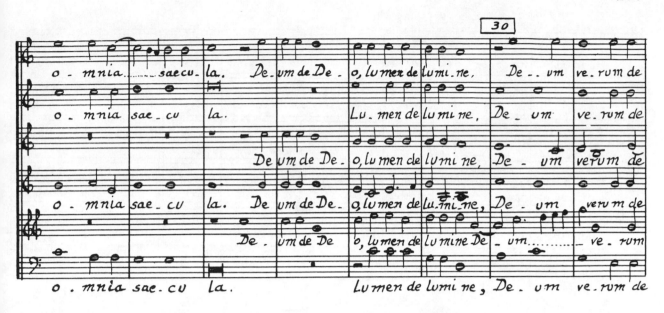

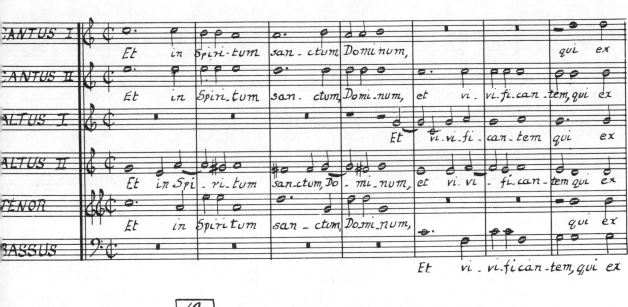

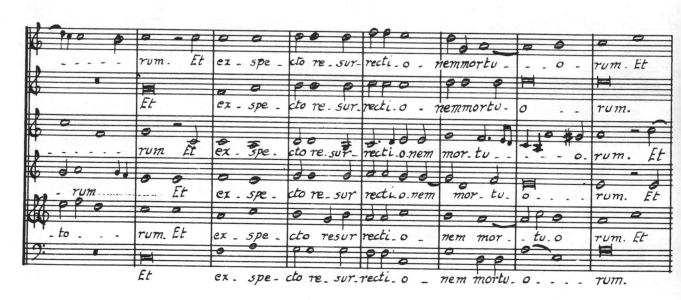

Sanctus

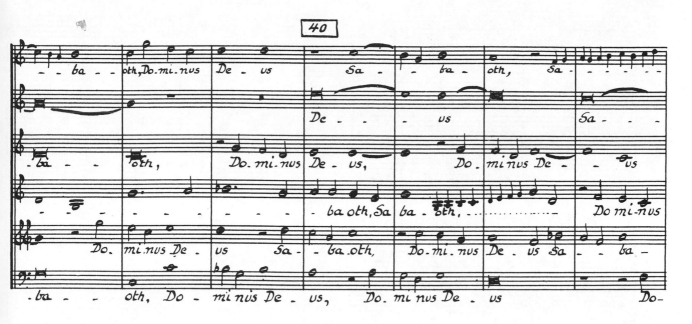

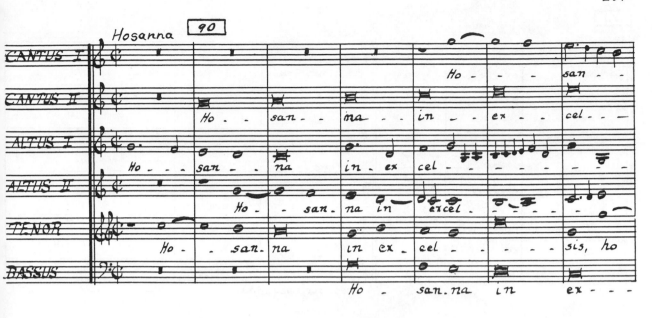

110

120

Benedictus

Agnus Dei I

Mass: Repleatur os meum laude.

Palestrina

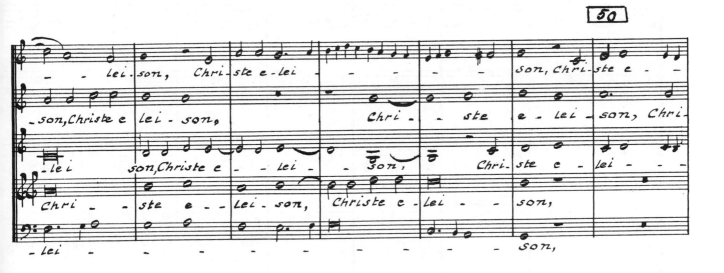

-son, Ky-rie e-lei - - - son, Ky - ri.e........ e.lei - - son,

-lei-son, Ky-ri-e........ e-lei-son,Ky.rie e - lei - - son,

- -son, Ky- ri-e-e.lei - son, Ky - ri.e e -

-lei-son,Ky-rie e - lei - son, Ky-ri-

Ky- ri.e................... e.lei - son, Ky - ri.e........ e-lei-

Ky-ri-e e-lei - -.son, Ky - ri-e e-lei- - son.

Ky-ri-e........ e-lei - - son.

-lei - - - son, Ky-ri-e e-leison,Ky-ri........ e - lei - - son.

-e.....e-lei - son,Ky-ri-e........ e-lei - - son.

- - - - - son, Ky.ri.e e - lei - - - son.

284

286

Hosanna

Benedictus

CANTUS

Be - nedictus qui ve -

ALTUS

Be - nedictus qui ve -

TENOR (I)

Be - ne.dictus qui ve - nit, be - ne.di.ctus qui..

- nit, be - ne.dictus qui ve -

- nit, be - ne.dictus qui re -

.... ve. nit, be - ne.dictus qui.......... ve - -

- nit, qui............ ve - - nit in nomi.

- nit, qui ve - - - - - - -

.nit, be - ne.dictus qui ve - - - - -

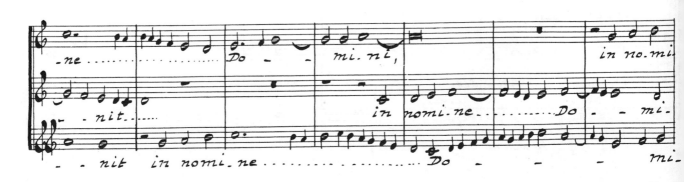

-ne............ Do - - mi.ni, in no.mi

- nit...... in nomi.ne............Do - mi.

- .nit in nomi.ne............... .... Do - - - mi.

Hosanna
ut supra.

Agnus Dei. I.

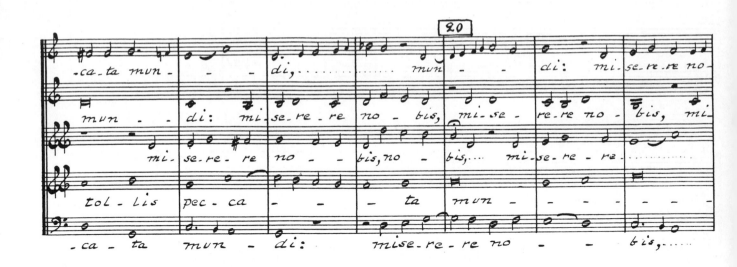

Agnus Dei. II

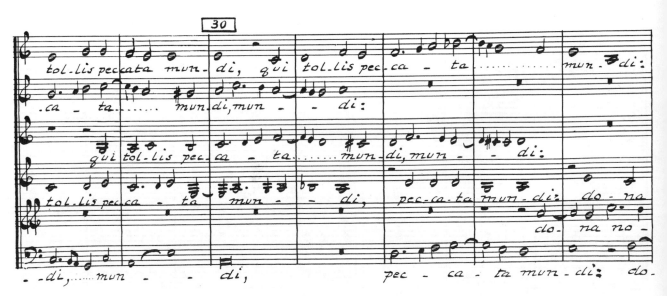

GREGORIAN CHANT

Gregorian chant, or plain song, is the name of unisonous ecclesiastical art music in use in the Christian Church of the West before the development of harmony, written on scales derived from the Greek modes.

The modes used in plain song were limited, quite early, to four authentic, (Dorian, Phrygian, Lydian, and Mixolydian), and four plagal (Hypodorian, Hypophrygian, Hypolydian, and Hypomixolydian) modes.

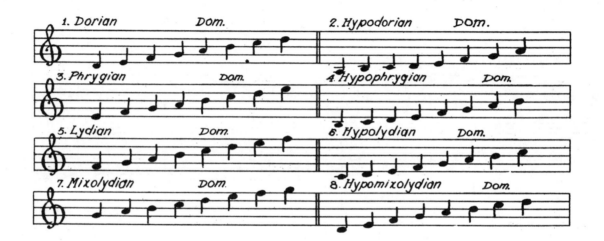

This modal system is different from that of the original Greek modes, due to some misunderstanding of the latter.

There are two main collections of Gregorian chant: the Gradual* and the Antiphonal. In the Gradual the chief ancient pieces are: the Introit, or Antiphona ad introitum, at the beginning of the service; the Gradual, with Alleluia or tract, which precede the Gospel; the Offertory which accompanies the preparation of the oblations; the Communion or antiphona ad Communionem which accompanies the partaking of the Sacrament.

In the parallel collection of music, the Antiphonal, we find the Responds which form musical interludes between the lessons and the Antiphons which form an integral part of the Psalmody. This collection is used mainly in the monasteries for the singing of the Office.

In both collections the modes are indicated by the numbers one to eight.

_____

*The most important parts of the Gradual and Antiphonal are available in modern notation (Liber Usualis).

The relation of plain song to measured music may be expressed thus: plain song is analogous to prose, and measured music, with its definite, generally regular, subdivisions of time, is analogous to poetry, with its definite subdivisions of metre.

Explanation of signs found in Gregorian chant:

 Ictus. The rhythmical ictus is an alighting or resting place sought by the rhythm at intervals of every two or three (eighth) notes. It does not mean accent or stress. The rhythm is one of the simplest, i.e., two or three eighth notes, their order of succession free.

Musical punctuation, in general corresponding to comma, semicolon, period.

∧ Pressus, a neum meaning a compact strong sound of double value, demanding, in many cases, some degree of acceleration on the preceding notes.

Distropha and tristropha, meaning a twice or thrice repeated vocal pulsation, very rapid in character, like a hand tapping (according to ancient authority).

V. Verse (from the psalms).

℟ Back to response.

i ii iij i, ii repeated; iij to be sung three times.

 Episema, meaning holding.

e u o u a e Saeculorum Amen (end of Gloria Patri).

* Asterisk meaning division of the choir according to previous agreement.

 Quilisma. The note or the group of notes immediately preceding the note below or above this sign must be prolonged. It appeared in the old notation as a jagged neume.

The above signs are all taken from the modern notation in Liber Usualis.

Page

1. Kyrie (sung after Introit).   Recorded by The Pius X School.   1
   See translation of mass.

2. Alleluia.   Recorded by the Solesmes Monks.
   Alleluia. V. The just shall spring as the lily; and shall flourish
   forever before the Lord. Alleluia.   1

3. Passer. Transposed chant, in which the first part belongs to the third   2
   tone and ends with a psalm cadence in the third tone; the second part is
   in the first tone. Notice the attempt at imitation of the cooing of the
   turtledove.

   The sparrow hath found herself a house, and the turtle a nest, where she
   may lay her young ones: thy altars, O Lord of hosts, my King, and my God:
   blessed are they that dwell in thy house, they shall praise thee for ever
   and ever.

4. Ad te levavi.   Recorded by the Solesmes Monks.   2
   To thee have I lifted up my soul. In thee, O my God, I put my trust: let
   me not be ashamed. Neither let my enemies laugh at me: for none of them
   that wait on thee shall be confounded.

5. Kyrie. In this ancient chant we find the old dominant b. Because of   2
   the frequent modification of b to b flat due to the tritone the dominant was later changed to c.

6. Sanctus. In this chant we find both the old and the new dominant.   3
   For translation, see mass.

7. Kyrie. Dominant on c only.   3

8. Alleluia. With modulation   3
   Alleluia. V. Come, O Lord, and do not delay; forgive the sins of thy
   people Israel. Alleluia.

9. Response.   Recorded by the Solesmes Monks.   4
   Behold how the Just dieth, and none taketh it to heart: and just men are
   taken off, and no one considereth: the Just is taken away from the face
   of iniquity: and his memory shall be in peace. V. He was dumb like the
   lamb before his shearer, and opened not His mouth: He was taken away
   from distress, and from judgment. R.

10. Sanctus.   Recorded by The Pius X School.   5

11. Agnus Dei.   Recorded by The Pius X School.   5

12. Antiphon. In the pure Lydian mode.   5
    Behold, the Lord will come, and with Him all His saints: and on that day
    there will be a great light, alleluia.

13. Gradual. The mode is mixed, i.e., it has both b and b flat. With   6
    modulation
    Princes sat, and spoke against me: and the wicked persecuted me: help
    me, O Lord, my God: Save me for thy mercy's sake.

14. Gradual. Benedictus. In the Lydian mode (mixed).   6

15. Communion.   Recorded by the Solesmes Monks.   7
    Christ our Pasch is immolated, alleluia: therefore let us feast with the
    unleavened bread of sincerity and truth. Alleluia, alleluia, alleluia.

16. Antiphon.
    Thou shalt sprinkle me with hyssop, O Lord, and I shall be cleansed; thou   7
    shalt wash me, and I shall be made whiter than snow. Ps.50. Have mercy
    on me, O God, according to thy great mercy. V. Glory be to the Father,
    and to the Son, and to the Holy Ghost. As it was in the beginning, is
    now, and ever shall be, world without end. Amen.

17. Gradual.   Recorded by the Solesmes Monks.   8
    Thou, O Lord, that sittest upon the Cherubim, stir up thy might, and
    come. V. Give ear, O thou that rulest Israel: thou that leadest Joseph
    like a sheep.

18. Offertory.   Recorded by the Solesmes Monks.   8
    Moses prayed in the sight of the Lord his God, and said: Why, O Lord, is
    thy indignation enkindled against thy people, Let the anger of thy mind
    cease; remember Abraham, Isaac, and Jacob, to whom thou didst swear to
    give a land flowing with milk and honey: and the Lord was appeased from
    doing the evil, which he had spoken of doing against his people.

19. Introit.   Recorded by the Solesmes Monks.   9
    The Spirit of the Lord hath filled the whole earth, alleluia; and that
    which containeth all things hath knowledge of the voice, alleluia, alle-
    luia, alleluia. Ps. 67. Let God arise, and let his enemies be scat-
    tered; and let them that hate him, flee from before his face. V. Glory.

Orlandus Lassus (1532-94).

    Cantiones duarum vocum. In all the modes used in ecclesiastical style.
    Texts from the Vulgate: 10

2-1. Eccl. 14:22.
    Blessed is the man that shall continue in wisdom, and that shall medi-
    tate in his justice, and in his mind shall think of the all seeing eye
    of God.

2-2. Proverbs 3: 13,14.   12
    Blessed is the man that findeth wisdom and is rich in prudence: The pur-
    chasing thereof is better than the merchandise of silver, and her fruit
    than the chiefest and purest gold.

Page
14

2-3. I Cor. 2:9.
That eye hath not seen, nor ear heard, neither hath it entered into the
heart of man, what things God hath prepared for them that love God.

2-4. Eccl. 39:6.   16
He will give his heart to resort early to the Lord that made him, and he
will pray in the sight of the most high.

2-5. Proverbs 10: 28,29.   18
The expectation of the just is joy; but the hope of the wicked shall
perish. The strength of the upright is the way of the Lord: and fear
to them that work evil.

2-6. John 8:12.   20
He that followeth me, walketh not in darkness but shall have the light
of life, sayeth the Lord.

2-7. Book of Wisdom 10:19.   22
The just took the spoils of the wicked, and they sung to thy holy name,
O Lord, and they praised with one accord thy victorious hand.

2-8. This is part of the responsory for Lesson VI in Matins for the Feast   24
of All Saints, Nov. 1.
My holy people, who in this world have known only toil and strife, I
shall grant to you the reward for all your labors.

2-9. Matthew 16:24.   26
If any man will come after me, let him deny himself, and take up his
cross, and follow me, sayeth the Lord.

2-10. Matthew 25:23.   28
Well done, good and faithful servant: because thou hast been faithful
over a few things I will place thee over many things: enter thou into
the joy of thy Lord.

2-11. Book of Wisdom 3:7. Matt. 13:43.   30
The just shall shine, and shall run to and fro like sparks among the
reeds.

2-12. Motet in honor of the Blessed Virgin Mary.   32
As a rose among thorns even to them its beauty lends,
So the Virgin Mary casts her grace and charm
Over all her progeny.   For from her has sprung
The Flower, whose fragrance is the gift of life.

Translation of the text of the Mass:
Kyrie eleison, Christe eleison, Kyrie eleison.
Lord, have mercy. Christ, have mercy. Lord, have mercy.

Gloria: Glory be to God on high (intoned by the priest).
Choir: And on earth peace to men of good will. We praise thee; we bless thee;
We adore thee; we glorify thee. We give thee thanks for thy great glory, O Lord,
heavenly King. God the Father Almighty. O Lord Jesus Christ, the only-begotten
Son: O Lord God, Lamb of God, Son of the Father, who taketh away the sins of the
world, have mercy on us: who taketh away the sins of the world, receive our
prayers: who sitteth at the right hand of the Father, have mercy on us. For
thou only art holy: thou only art Lord: thou only, O Jesus Christ, are most
high, together with the Holy Ghost, in the glory of God the Father, Amen.

Credo: I believe in one God (intoned by the priest).
Choir: The Father Almighty, maker of heaven and earth, and of all things visible
and invisible. And in one Lord Jesus Christ, the only begotten Son of God, born
of the Father before all ages; God of God, light of light, true God of true God;
begotten not made; consubstantial with the Father; by whom all things were made.
Who for us men, and for our salvation, came down from heaven; and was incarnate by
the Holy Ghost, of the Virgin Mary; and was made man. He was crucified also for
us, suffered under Pontius Pilate, and was buried. And the third day he rose
again according to the scriptures; and ascended into heaven. He sitteth at the
right hand of the Father; and he shall come again with glory to judge the living
and the dead; and his kingdom shall have no end, and in the Holy Ghost, the Lord
and giver of life, who proceedeth from the Father and the Son, who together with
the Father and the Son is adored and glorified; who spoke by the prophets. And
one holy catholic and apostolic church. I confess one baptism for the remission
of sins. And I await the resurrection of the dead, and the life of the world to
come. Amen.

Sanctus: Holy, holy, holy, Lord God of hosts. Heaven and earth are full of thy
glory. Hosanna in the highest.
Benedictus: Blessed is he that cometh in the name of the Lord.

Agnus Dei I: Lamb of God, who takest away the sins of the world, have mercy on
us.
Agnus Dei II: Lamb of God, who takest away the sins of the world, grant us peace.

    There are two Magnificats in each of the eight modes. This one has
    been selected because it is one of the few examples of the use of the
    pure Lydian mode. Notice the invariable final cadence on A. The com-
    position is fugal throughout. The following Gregorian chant is intoned
    at the beginning:

1.   Magnificat a - ni - ma me-a Do- mi-num

    The polyphonic treatment alternates with the chant according to the
    numbers.

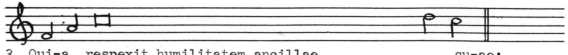

3. Qui-a respexit humilitatem ancillae   su-ae:
5. Et mi-sericor- dia ejus a progenie in   pro-geni-es
7. De- po-suit potentes de   se-de,
9. Sus-ce-pit Israel puerus   su-um,
11. Glo-ri-a Patri, et   Fili-o,

3. ecce enim ex hoc beatam me dicent omnes gene -ra -ti -o -nes
5. ti - - - - - - - - mentibus e-um.
7. et exal- - - - - - - ta -vit humiles.
9. recordatus miseri - - - - cor-diae su-ae.
11. et Spi - - - - - - - ri-tui sancte.

1. My soul doth magnify the Lord:
2. And my spirit hath rejoiced in God, my Savior.
3. For He hath regarded the lowliness of His handmaid:
   for behold, from henceforth, all generations shall call me
   blessed.
4. For He that is mighty, hath done great things to me: and holy is
   His name.
5. And His mercy is from generation to generations: unto them that
   fear Him.
6. He hath shown might in his arm: He hath scattered the proud in the
   conceit of their hearts.
7. He hath put down the mighty from their seat: and exalted the humble.
8. He hath filled the hungry with good things: and the rich He hath
   sent empty away.
9. He hath helpen Israel His servant: being mindful of His mercy.
10. As He spoke to our fathers: to Abraham and to His seed forever.
11. Glory be to the Father, to the Son, and to the Holy Ghost:
12. As it was in the beginning, is now, and ever shall be, world without
    end, Amen.

         In the Phrygian mode. On the Gregorian Hymn of the same
         name (see Liber usualis, p. 963).

      5-2 Petra Sancta 162
         In the Aeolian mode. Thematic origin unknown.

5-3, 5-4 Vestiva i Colli. 168, 173
         In the Dorian mode. On his own madrigal of the same name.

      5-5 Alleluia Tulerunt Dominum. 182
         In the Mixolydian mode.
         They have taken away my Lord, and I know not where they have
         laid him. If thou hast taken him away, tell me and I will
         take him away. (Mary Magdalen, following the resurrection.)
         Taken from John 20:13,15 (last portion of each verse)

      5-6 In Dominicis Quadragesima: Vesper hymn on the Gregorian theme . . 190
         "Ad preces nostras." Only the two last movements are used in
         this book.
         In the Aeolian mode. In the last movement the soprano and the sec-
         ond tenor form a canon at the octave.
         Grant to us a fountain of tears, the potent strength that comes
         from fasting; destroy with thy might (literally "sword") our
         thousand carnal vices.
         Glory be to God, the Father Eternal, and to thee, eternally be-
         gotten Son, with whom the Holy Spirit, (in all things) equal,
         reigneth forever.

    My heart hath expected reproach and misery; and I looked
    for one that could grieve together with Me, but there was
    none: I sought for one that would comfort Me, and I found
    none; and they gave me gall for my food, and in My thirst
    they gave Me vinegar to drink.

    I will exalt Thee. O Lord. for Thou hast upheld me,
    and hast not made mine enemies to rejoice over me:
    O Lord, I have cried to Thee, and Thou hast healed me.
              (Translation from the St. Andrew missal)

    Lord have mercy on us
    Christ hear us
    Christ graciously hear us
    God the Father of heaven, have mercy on us
    Holy Trinity, one God, have mercy on us.

    Holy Mary,   Pray for us
    Holy Virgin of virgins
    Mother of Christ   (Same response after such invoca-
    Mother most chaste   tion down to the "Agnus Dei")
    Mother most amiable
    Mother most faithful
    Virgin most merciful
    Refuge of sinners
    Comfortress of the afflicted

    Queen of Angels
    Queen of all Saints

    Lamb of God, who takest away the sins of the world, have mercy on us.

In the Mixolydian mode. In this mass Palestrina shows his
mastery of the contrapuntal devices of the Netherland
school. Canonic throughout, the Kyrie and the Hosanna show
two pairs of canons; the Benedictus a canon "trinitas in
unitate," i.e., three in one, and the five part Agnus Dei
the three upper voices are in three part canon, while the
two lower voices form a canon in two parts.

In the Mixolydian mode. L'Homme Arme, an old French Chan-
son used as canto fermo by a number of 15th and 16th century
masters in the composition of a mass called Missa L'Homme
Arme, the purpose of which was to show their skill and in-
genuity in the use of contrapuntal devices.

The above theme while not fully agreeing with the canti
fermi used by the composers previous to Palestrina, may
be accepted as the standard form. It is the version re-
sulting from joining the phrases as they appear in the
mass by Palestrina.

There are two editions of this mass: 1570 and 1599;
the first, in triple time, and the second, in $\frac{4}{2}$ time. The
curious fact about these two editions is that by changing
the triple time of the first edition to $\frac{4}{2}$ time by rebar-
ring it the result will be that of the 1599 edition with
every important cadence correctly placed.

In the Ionian mode. Also called the Hexachord Mass. Two
forms of the Guidonian hexachord are used; on C (hexachordum naturale), and on G (hexachordum durum). The hexachord
on F (hexachordum molle) is not used on account of its mod-
ulating properties.

In the Phrygian mode. A great example of the canonic art,
in all possible intervals. (The Gloria, in canon at the
fourth, and the Credo, in canon at the fifth, are omitted
in this book, since there are numerous other examples of
imitation in these intervals.)